O COME, O COME EMMANUEL

WAITING ON THE ADVENT WORD

A First Guide to Using Scripture in Groups

About the authors

Bill Redmond is a Roman Catholic priest of Liverpool archdiocese. After graduating in Modern Languages from Oxford University, he trained for the priesthood at Upholland College, Lancashire. Ordained priest in 1975, Bill subsequently pursued postgraduate studies in Scripture at the Biblical Institute in Rome and the École Biblique in Jerusalem. After a period of lecturing in Biblical Studies at Ushaw College, Durham, Bill is now Parish Priest of St Paul of the Cross, Burtonwood, near Warrington. He has maintained a particular interest in making the fruits of Old Testament and New Testament scholarship accessible to the non-specialist in the parish situation.

Paul Murray, of Newman College, Birmingham, was formerly an Adult Christian Educator for the Department of Pastoral Formation of the Archdiocese of Liverpool. Paul is a married lay man. He studied for an MA in Theology at Durham University and has a particular interest in developing methods of scripture study which enable non-specialists to understand the Bible for themselves.

O COME,
O COME EMMANUEL

WAITING ON THE ADVENT WORD

BILL REDMOND
AND PAUL MURRAY

 the bible reading fellowship

The Bible Reading Fellowship
Ground Floor
Warwick House
25 Buckingham Palace Road
London SW1W 0PP

First published 1990
© BRF 1990

British Library CIP data
Redmond, Bill
O come, O come Emmanuel.
1. Christian church. Advent & Christmas
I. Title   II. Murray, Paul, *1947–*
II. Bible Reading Fellowship
263.91

ISBN 0-900164-93-X

Drawings by Donald Mullis
Typeset by Cambridge Composing (UK) Ltd
Printed by Bocardo Press Ltd, Didcot

CONTENTS

PREFACE

Scripture study can sometimes be a dry, academic exercise with little relevance to our lives and world. It is also in danger of becoming a safe, pious exercise which does not move beyond oneself and one's own prayer life. In contrast, the authors of this book believe that scripture study should be an exciting, challenging and deeply creative encounter with the living Word of God. At the heart of this book is the conviction that we study scripture together so that in learning how God 'spoke' through the events of yesterday we can better understand how God is calling us today in our lives, communities and world. In *O Come, O Come Emmanuel – Waiting On The Advent Word* they have sought to provide a resource that will help to unlock the creative potential of the Word of God amongst us.

O Come, O Come Emmanuel is intended for group use during the Advent season. It consists of four scripture studies built around a sound adult education process. Each scripture study comes complete with leader's notes, additional background information, participants' worksheets (which may be photocopied) and suggested prayer material. The book also includes full training notes on how to use the scripture studies and detailed guidelines on how to develop further Bible studies based on the same method.

O Come, O Come Emmanuel may be used in a wide variety of contexts: with scripture groups; housegroups; ecumenical discussion groups; prayer groups; justice and peace groups; mothers' groups; readers' groups and Advent reflection groups. Practically anybody could lead a group using this material as no previous experience of leading scripture groups is presumed by the authors. They hope that it will introduce many to the joys of shared scripture study for the first time. The book will also be of great help to experienced scripture group leaders who are looking for fresh ideas and approaches.

This is a modest piece of work. However, it would never have seen the light of day without the encouragement, help and advice of a large number of people. In particular we would like to thank the intrepid band who braved hail and gales to attend the five evenings at Upholland College out of which this book has grown and those who led their first scripture study sessions using this material. Thanks also are due to Andrea Murray whose help with proof reading, design and production ensured that the material actually saw the light of day; to Chris Fallon, Maureen Knight and Pat Jones, of the Liverpool Archdiocesan Pastoral Formation Team, whose professional criticism and guidance proved invaluable; to Angela Norris and Kitty Anderson for their untiring assistance with printing and collating. Our thanks finally go to Dennis Napier, Michael King and all at Bible Reading Fellowship who have now made this material available to a far greater number than the co-authors ever dared to imagine.

Bill Redmond
Paul Murray   7th September 1990

INTRODUCTION

Why do we study scripture?

We study scripture because we believe that it is God's word to us. Through the events and experiences recorded in the Bible, people came to understand how God was present and active in their lives and world. The Bible records both these 'revelatory' events and the significance that our ancestors saw in them.

So we study scripture because we believe that in looking at how God was present and active, calling people *then*, we can understand better how God is present and active, calling us *today* in our lives, in our parish and in our nation and world.

How do we study scripture?

We believe that God's word is a living word that speaks to us today. So studying the scriptures is not a dry academic exercise. It engages our feelings and imaginations, our hopes and fears. We ask, '*What strikes us about this passage? What would the various characters have felt like?*'

When we say that the Bible is God's word to us, we do not mean that it came down ready-written from heaven. We believe that God was working in the real-life human situations and historical events that the Bible tells us about. We believe that the word of God was communicated to the writers of the Bible through these events and situations. They heard the word of God not as a word spoken from 'on high' but by reflecting on their lives and the life of their nation.

So if we want to hear God's word in scripture then we cannot just treat the Bible as a set of abstract, eternal truths. We have to go behind the words of the Bible, to try and understand the situations and experiences which they speak about. In this way we will learn how our ancestors understood God to be with them, active in their lives and world. We ask, '*What is the background to this passage of scripture?*'

In saying that the Bible is God's word, we do not mean that God just 'spoke' in special times in the past. We believe that God is still with us, involved in our lives, experience and world today. We do not study the Bible just to hear how God 'spoke' yesterday. We study scripture so that in learning how God 'spoke' through the events of yesterday we can better hear how God 'speaks' in our world today. We ask, '*How does this challenge us today – in our personal lives, in our parish, in our nation and world?*'

Taking these three points together, we can say that exploring scripture is a real relationship with the living word of God. This relationship involves:

- **Prayer, imagination and feelings;**
- **Learning about the background to the scriptures;**
- **Listening to our situation.**

These are the three foundation stones of scripture study/sharing.

Why this book?

There is an ever-increasing interest in scripture study. Many people have benefitted from prayerful ways of reading scripture, which have helped them to listen to what scripture is saying in their lives. However, people often feel far less confident about exploring the background of scripture passages. Again, some who have followed more 'academic' scripture courses feel confident about exploring the background to the written word but are unsure about how to use this knowledge in a living way which can speak to our situation.

There were a number of requests for an easy-to-use resource that brought these two sides together. Remember the three foundation stones that we mentioned on the previous page:

- **Prayer, imagination and feelings;**

  - **Learning about the background to the scriptures;**

    - **Listening to our situation**.

What better time for us to use such a pack together than during the Advent season when we prepare to welcome the living word of Christ into our lives afresh?

The Sessions

EACH SESSION FOLLOWS AN ADVENT READING:

Session 1 – Isaiah 7:10–15
   – Unto us a child is born, the messianic prophecies of Isaiah.

Session 2 – Matthew 2:13–18
   – The flight into Egypt, Matthew's infancy narrative.

Session 3 – Luke 1:5–17; 1:26–33
   – The annunciations of Jesus and John the Baptist, Luke's infancy narrative.

Session 4 – Luke 1:46–55
   – Mary's manifesto, the Magnificat.

EACH SESSION FOLLOWS THE SAME PATTERN:

1. Welcome   (*5 mins*)
- Introduction to the theme of the evening and opening prayer

2. Short involving exercise   (*5 mins*)
- To take us into the theme of the evening

3. Hear the Word   (*5 mins*)
- We listen as the scripture passage is read rather than following it on the page.
Take it in turns to read the passage.

4. Feel the Word   (*20 mins*)
- We reflect on the passage and ask:
What strikes us?
What does the passage say to us?
What would the characters in the story have felt like?
Why did they act in the way that they did?

5. Explore the Word   (*30 mins*)
- We explore the background to the scripture passage using the suggested notes. We ask:
Does this help us at all?
Does it open up any new insights?

6. Responding to the Word   (*25 mins*)
- We focus on our own situation and ask:
How does the Word speaks to our situation?
How does it challenge us
     – as individuals?
     – as parish?
     – as nation?
What action or changes does this call us to make as individuals and as community?

7. Prayer   (*10 mins*)
- reading,
- quiet time/music,
- focal point: slide, picture, 'holy table',
- do something together.

Helpful hints for leading scripture groups

* Do make sure that someone has taken care of arranging the venue, organizing refreshments and arranging publicity or invitations.

* Do read over the session and prepare yourself beforehand.

* Do pay attention to the atmosphere of the room:
  Is it starchy and formal or relaxed and informal?
  What is the heating, lighting, seating like?

* Do make sure people know each other's names!

* Do make sure that everyone can see and hear everyone else.

* Do encourage people to listen and to share what they think.

* Do show people that what they say is helpful and accepted.

* Do encourage people to tell their own stories.

* Do be prepared to share your own ideas and opinions.

* Do show respect when questioning other people's ideas and opinions.

* Do thank everybody for taking part.

* Do join in any follow-up action.

* Don't forget to ask people to bring along a Bible.

* Don't start late or run over time.

* Don't worry about disagreement – accept it because different viewpoints are all valid.

* Don't let the discussion drift too far away from the theme.

* Don't put pressure on anyone to speak, but do invite them with a word or gesture or look.

* Don't talk too much yourself.

* Don't allow anyone to dominate the discussion.

* Don't panic if it goes quiet – people might be thinking!

* Don't think that you need to have all the answers. A group leader does not need to be an expert. The best group leaders are those who help the people in their group to be at ease and able to share together.

SESSION 1: Leader's Notes

1. Welcome   *(5 mins)*

Make sure that you begin this first session by welcoming everyone. A cup of tea or coffee on arrival will help to create an inviting atmosphere. Make sure you start on time. You may like to begin by saying something like:

'Welcome to our first evening together exploring the Advent readings. There are four evenings in this series and tonight we are going to look at one of the readings from the first Sunday of Advent. It is a reading that we are all very familiar with from the prophet Isaiah. There is a phrase that "familiarity breeds contempt". Whilst that is probably a bit strong, it is true that when we become familiar with hearing certain passages from scripture, we think that we have them summed up, that there is no more to them. This short series is an opportunity to explore the richness of these familiar readings, to explore what the original writers meant and to listen to how these readings continue to challenge us and to hold a promise for us today.'

'Perhaps we could begin by introducing ourselves.'
(Do a 'round robin' in which people introduce themselves in turn and say why they decided to be part of the Advent Scripture Group. This may be impractical if the numbers of people exceed 15–20 and it may be inappropriate if everyone already knows everyone else very well.)

'Let's begin with a prayer.'

> Lord our God,
> help us to prepare
> for the coming of Christ your Son.
> May he find us waiting,
> eager in joyful prayer.
>
> We ask this through our Lord Jesus
>   Christ, your Son,
> who lives and reigns with you and the
>   Holy Spirit,
> one God, for ever and ever.

2. Involving exercise   *(5 mins)*

'Let's move on . . . I would like to ask how many of us are motorists?'

What do you do when you see a red light or an amber light?

How do you know when people are crossing the road nearby?

Imagine that you could not read. How could you tell that you were joining the motorway?

If no one is willing to volunteer an answer in the large group, invite them to have a word with their neighbour and then invite a few reactions. People will probably mention 'looking', 'seeing', 'signs'. Acknowledge these comments and say: 'The passage that we are exploring tonight is concerned with a sign and what that sign meant. Let's listen to the word.'

3. Hear the word (5 mins)

The text is read by someone you invited to read at the start of the evening. Invite the other members of the group to listen to the word as it is read. (The text is printed out on the worksheets.)

After the word has been read, give the worksheets out and invite people to read the passage again to themselves. Ask them to read the passage slowly, to imagine how the various characters felt and to think of who they identify with.

4. Feel the word (20 mins)

Invite people to turn their chairs round into groups of threes and fours. Ask them to spend a quarter of an hour reflecting together on the questions under the heading *FEEL THE WORD* on their worksheets.

What words, phrases or images strike you in this passage?
Which character do you identify with? Why?

What do you feel about Ahaz refusing to ask for a sign and Isaiah insisting that he would receive one?
What does the notion of a SIGN say to you?

Encourage the groups to share their feelings and reactions, and to avoid getting bogged down in discussion.

After the informal groups have shared on these questions for 15 minutes call them back together and invite people to share in the larger group what they were saying in their small group. Keep the responses fairly brief and try not to get sidetracked into discussion. Spend no more than five minutes on this.

5. Explore the word (30 mins)

'Let's look at the background to this passage and see what the prophet Isaiah meant when he wrote it. There are a few points that may be helpful:'

The leader then gives a *short* talk covering the points laid out in the suggested input below. This is only a *suggested* input; it would be best if you adapted it and made it your own rather than reading it out as it stands. You will find some further background information at the end of these leader's notes which you may like to look at. Keep your input to 5–10 minutes maximum.

This passage tells us of events that took place about 735 BC. King Ahaz has recently become King of Judah. He is no shakes at politics or prayer! At this point of the story (which is historical fact) he has done a deal with his enemies the Assyrians. This is bad politics (it won't work); and bad faith (it will let Assyrian idolatry in by the back door).

Obstinate Ahaz will not listen to the Lord. Pretending to be pious, he refuses to ask for a sign, but this is not piety; it is faithlessness. At verse 13 Isaiah (who is the speaker) loses his temper because Ahaz is, as he puts it, 'wearying God'. Like it or not, Ahaz will have a sign.

The next bit is very familiar. But be careful . . . The original Hebrew word – *alma* – normally means 'young woman' rather than 'virgin'. So this very special verse is more than a prophecy, made 700 years in advance, that the Blessed Virgin would conceive the Lord Jesus. Verse 15 makes this even clearer. The prophet is referring to an immediate historical figure who would 'eat curds and honey', i.e. bring a time of political stability and religious fervour to the kingdom of Judah.

Note: We call this 'layering':

  i. The prophet is familiar with the events of 735 BC.
 ii. The prophet warns of an immediate and humanly foreseeable change of events, i.e. the birth of a child.
iii. The prophet, under inspiration of the Holy Spirit, foretells an event of infinitely greater importance (i.e. the virginal conception of Jesus by Mary).

Invite people to return to their informal groups and to share their reactions to the input using the questions under *EXPLORE THE WORD*.

Do these points help explain the passage at all?
Do they open up any new insights?

After they've been discussing in groups for

about 15 minutes call everyone back to the large group and take any responses for a few minutes.

6. Responding to the word   *(25 mins)*

Ask people to turn their chairs round again and to share on the questions under *RESPONDING TO THE WORD* on the worksheets:

When we pray, how do we listen to what God is calling us to do rather than just 'wearying God' with our words?
What are the main signs of the times in our own town and world today?
What actions or changes does this word call us to make as individuals and communities? How can we bring this time of 'curds and honey' nearer? How can we share it with others?

After about 20 minutes draw the group together and invite any sharing in the wider group for a few minutes.

7. Prayer

Ask someone to read the following passage written by Archbishop Romero:

The True Christmas

No one can celebrate a genuine Christmas without being truly poor. The self-sufficient, the proud, those who, because they have everything, look down on others, those who have no need even of God – for them there will be no Christmas. Only the poor, the hungry, those who need someone to come on their behalf, will have that someone. That someone is God, Emmanuel, God-with-us. Without poverty of spirit there can be no abundance of God.

Have a few minutes quiet, maybe with some background music. A focal point is often helpful – a picture, a candle or a 'holy table'.

Finish by doing something together – singing a hymn or saying a prayer. You may like to use the following meditation by Bishop Helder Camara. It appears on the worksheets. You could ask people to think about it quietly for a few minutes and then to say it together.

Are we so deaf
that we do not hear
a loving God warning us
that humanity is in danger of
    committing suicide?

Are we so selfish
that we do not hear the just God
    demanding that we
do all we can
to stop injustice
suffocating the world
and driving it to war?

Are we so alienated
that we can worship God
at ease in luxurious temples
which are often empty
in spite of all their liturgical pomp
and fail to see,
    hear
    and serve God
where he is present
and where he requires OUR
    presence
among humankind,
    the poor,
    the oppressed,
    the victims of injustice
in which we ourselves are often
    involved?

It is not difficult
to do more than offer an emotional
    response,
sorrow and regret.
It is even more difficult
to give up our comfort,
break with old habits,
let ourselves be moved by grace,
and change our life
    – be converted.
Dom Helder Camara

'Good night. Safe home. See you next week!'

Additional background notes for the leader:

Who was Isaiah?

The prophet Isaiah, whose name actually means 'God will save', was born in Jerusalem in the early part of the 700s BC. He was called to the prophetic office about the year 745 BC and was around 35 at the time. Isaiah himself tells us that he was married to a prophetess and had two sons. His writings show him as a man of culture, a great poet with lofty ideas and an admirable command of language. Further, he was as courageous as he was cultured. Above all, his entire prophetic ministry was driven by his personal experience of the holiness of God.

The time and place

It is helpful to remember that at the time when Isaiah preached (745–687 BC) the ancient Promised Land had been split into two rival Kingdoms. The Northern Kingdom was still called Israel; and the Southern Kingdom was named Judah, with its capital in Jerusalem. Judah had grown extremely wealthy in the prophet's early lifetime, but, sadly, this prosperity had quickly become the cause of moral and social corruption. This situation is very familiar to us today, of course. Perhaps, many readers also know of the prophet Amos' struggle to promote social justice in the midst of wealth and greed.

A political danger with grave spiritual implications arose in 735 BC, at the beginning of the reign of King Ahaz. Ahaz was willing to do a political 'deal' with one of his most powerful neighbours, Assyria. On balance, this didn't benefit Judah very much. But what was infinitely worse was that it opened Judah's back door to the idolatrous cult of the Assyrians. Throw in the fact that King Ahaz was anything but a devout servant of God, and you can see what the prophet was up against.

The message

In the first place Isaiah, like Amos before him, had to undertake a nationwide moral crusade. He resolutely attacked social injustice, pinpointing it as the tell-tale sign of the Chosen People's shallow faith. 'Believe in the all powerful, all holy God,' he told his hearers, 'and next behave publicly and privately according to that belief. Then you will be assured of God's blessing.'

It should not surprise us that this divine favour was understood, at least partly, as *political*. 'Religion' and 'politics' were interlocked and a devout prophet, like Isaiah, was equally a capable politician. He clearly grasped the political situation of his time. Besides, with the help of the Holy Spirit, he could see that the only way to overcome all difficulties was to place unshakeable faith in God and in the one whom God would send. For Isaiah, this was God's Messiah (i.e. 'anointed one'). By ruling with a justice and peace previously undreamt of, he would establish a perfect harmony between all things. The peak of Isaiah's message is this: A Saviour would come and his advent would herald the beginning of a new age – *The Messianic age*.

SESSION 1: Worksheet

The Lord spoke to Ahaz again and said:

> Ask the Lord your God for a sign, either in the depths of Sheol or in the heights above.

But Ahaz said, 'I will not ask. I will not put the Lord to the test.' He then said:

> Listen now, House of David:
> are you not satisfied with trying human patience
> that you should try my God's patience too?
> The Lord will give you a sign in any case:
> It is this: the young woman is with child
> and will give birth to a son
> whom she will call Immanuel.
> On curds and honey will he feed
> until he knows how to refuse the bad
> and choose the good.

Feel the word

What words, phrases or images strike you in this passage?

Which character do you identify with? Why?

What do you feel about Ahaz refusing to ask for a sign and Isaiah insisting that he would receive one?

What does the notion of a SIGN say to you?

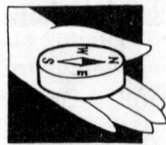

Explore the word

Do these points help explain the passage at all?

Do they open up any new insights?

From *O come, O come Emmanuel* © Bible Reading Fellowship 1990

Responding to the word

When we pray, how do we listen to what God is calling us to do rather than just 'wearying God' with our words?

What are the main signs of the times in our own town and world today?

What actions or changes does this word call us to make as individuals and communities?

How can we bring this time of 'curds and honey' nearer? How can we share it with others?

Prayer

We focus on the presence of the Lord amongst us and have a few moments of quiet. A passage will be read, followed by some more quiet.

Reflect quietly on the following passage by Bishop Helder Camara. After a few minutes we will finish by all saying it together.

Are we so deaf
that we do not hear
a loving God warning us
that humanity is in danger of
      committing suicide?

Are we so selfish
that we do not hear the just God
      demanding that we
do all we can
to stop injustice
suffocating the world
and driving it to war?

Are we so alienated
that we can worship God
at ease in luxurious temples
which are often empty
in spite of all their liturgical pomp
and fail to see,
      hear
      and serve God
where he is present
and where he requires OUR
      presence
among humankind,
      the poor,
      the oppressed,
      the victims of injustice
in which we ourselves are often
      involved?

It is not difficult
to do more than offer an emotional
      response,
sorrow and regret.
It is even more difficult
to give up our comfort,
break with old habits,
let ourselves be moved by grace,
and change our life
      – be converted.
Dom Helder Camara

SESSION 2: Leader's Notes

1. Welcome (5 mins)

Welcome people back to the second evening in the series, particularly any new faces: 'Tonight we are going to explore the passage from Matthew's gospel about the holy family fleeing to Egypt.'

'Let's begin with a prayer.'

Father in heaven,
the day draws near when the glory of
   your Son
will make radiant the night of the
   waiting world.

May the lure of greed not impede us
   from the joy
which moves the hearts of those who
   seek him.
May the darkness not blind us
to the vision of wisdom
which fills the minds of those who find
   him.

We ask this in the name of Jesus the
   Lord.

2. Involving exercise (5 mins)

Begin by reading the short passage printed below which was written by a woman from El Salvador:

Like Mary, I Too Had to Flee

Like Mary, I too had to flee when they persecuted my family. They cut my husband and two older sons to pieces, accusing them of learning communism from Catholic religious education classes. I left my home with my other three children and walked and walked until a *compadre* brought me here. I think that Mary deeply understands the mothers of our country because she underwent what we are suffering today. She now pleads with her son for our children when we no longer have the strength to do so. And she joins her voice to that of Archbishop Romero when she declares in her Magnificat that the rich will no longer oppress the lowly.

'Let us imagine for a few moments what it must be like for a young couple fleeing with a child in their arms from armed guards in China or El Salvador . . .'

Invite people to think about this for a minute and then to share with their neighbours. Then take reactions and comments from the group as a whole.

3. Hear the word   (*5 mins*)

This evening's passage (see worksheet) is read aloud. Invite people to listen to the word as it is read rather than following it on the sheet.

After the word has been read, give the worksheets out and invite people to read the passage again to themselves. Ask them to read the passage slowly, to imagine how the various characters felt and to think of who they identify with.

4. Feel the word   (*20 mins*)

Invite people to turn their chairs round into groups of threes and fours to reflect on the questions on the worksheet under the heading *FEEL THE WORD*. Encourage the groups to share their feelings and reactions.

What strikes us most about this passage?
Can you sense the tension and the fear, even panic, that the evangelist is trying to create?
Which characters are most appealing?
Which do you dislike?

After the informal groups have shared on these questions for a quarter of an hour call them back together. For a few minutes, invite people to share in the larger group what they were saying in their small group.

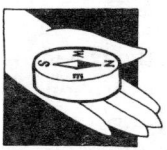

5. Explore the word   (*30 mins*)

'Let's look at the background to this passage and see what Matthew meant when he wrote it. There are a few points that may be helpful:'

As with last week, the leader gives a *short* talk covering the points laid out in the suggested input below. Try to adapt this input and to make it your own rather than reading it out as it stands. You will find some further background information at the end of these leader's notes which you may like to look at. Keep your input to between five and ten minutes.

The flight into Egypt and the Massacre of the Innocents warned that Jesus' life is already under threat from the insanely jealous Herod. Joseph escapes to Egypt with Mary and the new-born child. When the wise men did not report back as expected, Herod realized that he'd been taken for a ride. In a fit of rage, which was quite in character, Herod the Great initiated a scorched-earth policy. If he couldn't have Jesus alive, he'd have him dead.

Note the skill of Matthew's characterization: the vicious Herod; the caring, concerned Joseph; the vulnerable infant whose mother is scarcely less at risk. And, just off stage, the wily Magi who'd got one up on Herod.

We need to open the Old Testament to penetrate Matthew's message more deeply. At verse 15 he quotes the prophet Hosea (11:1) 'Out of Egypt I will call my son.' This is a touching reference by Hosea to Israel as the Lord's 'son'. Remember how in Exodus the youthful Moses fled for safety from Egypt and the Lord brought Israel, his people, out of their slavery in the land of Egypt. Matthew loosely mixes the two ideas here, and shows God protecting his Son, as he did Moses from a very early age, as well as rescuing his son from any possibility of enslavement to the heathen tyrant Herod. (Yes, Herod is meant to remind us of Pharaoh!) Finally, at verse 18, Matthew quotes Jeremiah 31:15. Rachel who died in childbirth (Genesis 35:16–20), wept for children that never were. She was buried near Bethlehem. Ramah is near Jerusalem and was the scene of national grief inflicted by an enemy.

The evangelist's point is clear. This attempted assault on the life of the child Jesus is a national religious catastrophe for Israel. There is more than a hint of Calvary here.

Invite people to return to their informal groups and to share their reactions to the input by focusing on the questions under *EXPLORE THE WORD.*

Do these points help explain the passage at all?
Do they open up any new insights?

After they've been discussing in groups for about 15 minutes call everyone back to the large group and take any responses for a few minutes.

6. Responding to the word (*25 mins*)

Ask people to turn their chairs around again and to share on the following questions:

What does this say to our situation?
Herod's insecurity and jealousy lead to violence. Can that happen to us also?
Who are the vulnerable and weak in our society?
How can we welcome the homeless and immigrants to our Christmas table?
How can we begin to fight against the tyranny of modern-day Herods?

After about 20 minutes draw the group together again and invite a short sharing in the wider group.

7. Prayer

Invite people to take a moment to quieten down. Ask them to put any papers on the floor.

Somebody reads the following passage by Thomas Merton:

> 'Into this world, this demented inn, in which there is absolutely no room for Him at all, Christ has come uninvited. But because He cannot be at home in it, because He is out of place in it, His place is with those who do not belong, who are rejected by power because they are regarded as weak, those who are discredited, who are denied the status of persons, who are tortured, bombed, and exterminated. With those for whom there is no room, Christ is present in the world. He is mysteriously present in those for whom there seems to be nothing but the world at its worst . . . It is in these that He hides Himself, for whom there is no room.'
>
> from *Raids on the Unspeakable*

Have a few minutes' quiet. Invite people to take it in turns to read the lines of the following poem.

> Like your landlord
> becoming your lodger:
>
> Like your managing director
> up before you for an interview:
>
> Like Beethoven
> queuing up for a ticket to his own concert:
>
> Like Picasso
> painting by numbers:
>
> God lived among us.

Invite people to continue this poem with their own phrases if they wish . . .

Finish by someone reading the following litany slowly. After each line we pause and all respond: ***Lord have mercy.***

> For those who grasp their prison bars
>   helplessly,
>   that we may walk free
> For those who rot in the dark
>   so that we may walk in the sun
> For those whose ribs have been
>   broken
>   so that we may breathe our fill
> For those whose backs have been
>   broken
>   so that we may walk erect
> For those whose faces have been
>   slapped
>   so that we may walk in fear of no
>   hand
> For those whose mouths have been
>   gagged
>   so that we may speak out
> For those whose pride lies in rags on
>   the slabs of their jails
>   so that we may proudly walk
> For those whose spouses live in
>   anguish
>   so that our spouses may live
>   happy
> For those whose country is in chains
>   so that our country may be free
> And for their jailers and for their
>   torturers . . .

'Good night. Safe home. See you next week!'

23

Additional background notes for the leaders:

Who was Matthew?
Open the New Testament and you will find the gospel according to St Matthew given first place in the batting-order. Why? Is this the first gospel and, moreover, one written by an actual disciple of the Lord? Appealing though this may sound, we need to be on our guard against jumping to conclusions.

A possible scenario would be as follows. Matthew the apostle may have pieced together a short and continuous narrative describing the major events of Jesus' public ministry and preaching. The early Christians seem to have known of this primitive work of Matthew, and as a result the 'Gospel according to St Matthew' came to be accorded a place of honour among the four gospels. In a nutshell, what was *thought* to be the earliest gospel was placed first in the ordering of the New Testament books.

However, strictly speaking, what Matthew the tax-collector wrote were probably just jottings; we can be pretty certain that he didn't write a fully-fledged 'gospel' as we now understand that word. So, while our gospel according to St Matthew may well be related to the apostle's original 'notes', the gospel of Matthew that we read now is a much later, and theologically more sophisticated, work.

Who wrote the gospel we still have? Again, we don't know. With caution we can say this: it was written in Greek, by an unknown member of a Jewish-Christian community. Sections may perhaps be translations of the apostle's original 'notes', but here again we are long on guesswork and short on hard facts!

The time and place
Our unknown evangelist must have been a teacher within a Christian community in Palestine some time between 75 and 100 AD. The phrases he uses, the religious customs he mentions and, above all, the theological emphasis of his gospel, all help to frame the drama of our Lord's ministry and death within a predominantly Jewish-Christian outlook. Matthew is deeply conscious of belonging to a well-defined community, a new-yet-old community. This community is the church, which is described as the fulfiller and fulfilment of God's will as disclosed in the Old Testament.

The message
In Matthew's manual of Christian teaching, Jesus is set forth as Israel's Messiah in whom God's purpose culminates, and by whose words and life his followers, the true Israel, may gain divine forgiveness. In this work of catechesis Matthew was trying to encourage his young Jewish-Christian community and to show the Jewish people how badly mistaken they had been in rejecting Jesus as the Messiah. His use of Old Testament quotations is central to both these aims. The life of Jesus, when seen in the light of prophecy and interpreted by faith, was not just a series of past events which a historian might record. It was the great turning point in God's plan to save mankind. Sadly, the Jewish people had failed to recognize him but this very rejection of Jesus by his own people had allowed the gospel message to spread to the entire world.

So, in Matthew's gospel, the life of Jesus is presented as a drama. Its prologue is the infancy gospel (chapters 1–2) which encapsulates in advance both the *sorrow* and the *glory* of the *rejected* and *risen* Messiah. While Joseph welcomes the child in the name of Israel and the House of David, Jerusalem, Judea and Herod reject him, persecute him and seek to kill him.

SESSION 2: Worksheet

Feel the word

What strikes you most about this passage?

Can you sense the tension and fear, even panic, that the evangelist is trying to create?

Which characters are most appealing?
And which are most appalling?

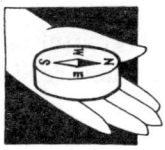

Explore the word

Do these points help explain the passage at all?

Do they open up any new insights?

Responding to the word

What does this say to our situation?

Herod's insecurity and jealousy lead to violence. Can that happen to us also?

After they had left, suddenly the angel of the Lord appeared to Joseph in a dream and said, 'Get up, take the child and his mother with you, and escape into Egypt, and stay there until I tell you, because Herod intends to search for the child and do away with him.' So Joseph got up and, taking the child and his mother with him, left that night for Egypt, where he stayed until Herod was dead. This was to fulfil what the Lord had spoken through the prophet:

I called my son out of Egypt.

Herod was furious on realising that he had been fooled by the wise men, and in Bethlehem and its surrounding district he had all the male children killed who were two years old or less, reckoning by the date he had been careful to ask the wise men. Then were fulfilled the words spoken through the prophet Jeremiah:

A voice is heard in Ramah,
lamenting and weeping bitterly:
it is Rachel weeping for her children,
refusing to be comforted
because they are no more.

Who are the vulnerable and weak in our society?

How can we 'welcome the homeless and immigrants to our Christmas table'?

How can we begin to fight against the tyranny of modern-day Herods?

Prayer

We have a time of quiet to focus ourselves on the presence of the Lord. A short reading is read.

After another short time of quiet, each person in turn reads a verse of the following poem.

Like your landlord
becoming your lodger:

Like your managing director
up before you for an interview:

Like Beethoven
queuing up for a ticket to his own
    concert:

Like Picasso
painting by numbers:

God lived among us.

If anyone wishes to make up a line to continue the poem, they do so . . .

Someone will read the following litany. After each line we pray: '*Lord have mercy*'.

For those who grasp their prison bars
    helplessly,
    that we may walk free
For those who rot in the dark
    so that we may walk in the sun
For those whose ribs have been
    broken
    so that we may breathe our fill
For those whose backs have been
    broken
    so that we may walk erect
For those whose faces have been
    slapped
    so that we may walk in fear of no
    hand
For those whose mouths have been
    gagged
    so that we may speak out
For those whose pride lies in rags on
    the slabs of their jails
    so that we may proudly walk
For those whose spouses live in
    anguish
    so that our spouses may live
    happy
For those whose country is in chains
    so that our country may be free
And for their jailers and for their
    torturers . . .

From *O come, O come Emmanuel* © Bible Reading Fellowship 1990

SESSION 3: Leader's Notes

1. Welcome   (*5 mins*)

Welcome people back to the third evening in the series: 'Tonight we are going to explore the passages in Luke's gospel about the birth of John the Baptist and the birth of Jesus.'

'Let's begin with a prayer.'

God of love and mercy,
help us to follow the example of Mary,
always ready to do your will.
At the message of an angel
she welcomed your eternal Son
and, filled with the light of your Spirit,
she became the temple of your Word,
who lives and reigns with you and the
     Holy Spirit,
one God, for ever and ever.

3. Hear the word   (*5 mins*)

Ask a man to read Luke 1:5–17. After a short pause, have a woman read Luke 1:26–33

After the word has been read, give the worksheets out and invite people to read the passages again to themselves. Ask them to read the passages slowly, to imagine how the various characters felt and to think of who they identify with.

2. Involving exercise   (*5 mins*)

'What has been good news for you this week? – Have a word with your neighbour . . .' Then take comments from the group as a whole.

4. Feel the word   (*20 mins*)

Invite people to turn their chairs round into groups of threes and fours to reflect on the questions that they will find on the worksheets under *FEEL THE WORD*. Encourage the groups to share their feelings and reactions.

What strikes you most about the passage?

Who do you feel more sympathy for: Elizabeth or Mary?

How must Mary have felt?

What do the words 'You have found favour with God' say to you?

After about a quarter of an hour, call everyone back together and invite people to spend a few minutes sharing what they were saying in their small group. Try and keep the responses fairly brief.

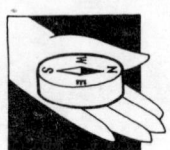

5. Explore the word   (*30 mins*)

'Let's look at the background to this passage and see what Luke meant when he wrote it. There are a few points that may be helpful:'

The Leader than gives a *short* talk covering the points laid out in the *suggested* input below. This does not need to be longer than about five to ten minutes.

A basic pattern is discernible in a large number of annunciation and nativity stories to be found throughout the Old Testament.

They generally exhibit seven elements:

i) The barrenness of the mother.

ii) A heavenly assurance that, by divine intervention, she will give birth.

iii) The consecration of the child to God.

iv) The naming of the child.

v) Some liturgical statement of praise.

vi) An act of presentation/dedication.

vii) A concluding statement of the child's subsequent high standing in the sight both of God and men.

Quite intentionally, Luke incorporates two annunciation stories into his Infancy Narrative. The story of Jesus' annunciation in the second passage is meant to be read in the light of the story of John the Baptist's annunciation in the first. Luke puts these two stories in parallel with each other: the coming of both is announced by the Angel Gabriel; the birth of both is described; their respective circumcision ceremonies are described; and reference is made to the hidden life of both.

It is valuable to perform a more detailed comparison of the two accounts in order to see how consistent and how close this parallelism is:

The Annunciation to Zechariah (1:5–25)	The Annunciation to Mary (1:26–38)
Scene: Zech and Elizabeth *vv. 5–6* **Enter:** The Angel Gabriel *v. 11* **Reaction:** fear on Zech's part *v. 12* **Promise:** Elizabeth to bear a son *v. 13b* **Prophecy:** he will be great *v. 15a* **Mission:** John's task is described *v. 17*	**Scene:** Mary and Joseph *v. 27* **Enter:** The Angel Gabriel *v. 26* **Reaction:** fear on Mary's part *v. 29* **Promise:** 'you will . . . bear a son' *v. 31a* **Prophecy:** 'He will be great' *v. 32a* **Mission:** Jesus's task is described *vv 32b–33*

The parallelism is meant to give a sense of gradual climax. The conscious repetitions in the second annunciation narrative are meant to underline a statement which will come from John the Baptist's lips later in the gospel: 'he who is mightier than I is coming . . .' (3:16).

Such close comparison of the details of each text shows how successful is Luke's technique of putting one text in parallel with another. He builds one very similar text upon another, while exploiting the differences between each to achieve an unmistakable climax.

Invite people to return to their informal groups and to share their reactions to the input.

Do these points help explain the passages at all?
Do they open any new insights?

After they have been discussing in groups for about 15 minutes call everyone back to the large group and take a few responses.

6. Responding to the word *(25 mins)*

Ask people to turn their chairs around again and to share on the questions under *RESPONDING TO THE WORD* on their worksheets.

Both passages speak of a fearful awareness of God's presence. Do you ever feel like this?
Mary's faith in God's power is astounding. Are you confident of God's power in your life?
Look again at the description of Mary's Son in verses 32 and 33 ('He will be great . . . no end'). Are we ready to welcome that kind of Saviour this Christmas?
How can we make steps to put 'Christ' back into 'Christmas'?
What do Elizabeth and Mary teach us of the dignity of women?

After 20 minutes or so, draw the group together again and invite any sharing for about 5 minutes.

7. Prayer

Invite people to put down any papers and to collect their thoughts for a moment. Somebody reads the passage '**Who am I?**' which is printed below:

> I am a woman
>   I am Filipino
>   I am alive
>   I am struggling
>   I am hoping.
>
> I am created in the image of God
> just like all other people in the world;
> I am a person with worth and dignity.
> I am a thinking person, a feeling
>   person, a doing person.
> I am the small I am that stands before
>   the big I AM.

I am a worker who is constantly challenged and faced with the needs of the church and society in Asia and in the global community.

I am angered by the structures and powers that create all forms of oppression, exploitation and degradation.

I am a witness to the moans, tears, banners and clenched fists of my people.

I can hear their liberating songs, their hopeful prayers and decisive march towards justice and freedom.

I believe that all of us – women and men
young and old, Christians and all others –
are called upon to do responsible action;
to be concerned
to be involved
NOW!
I am hoping
   I am struggling
      I am alive
         I am Filipino
            I am a woman.

Have a few minutes' quiet. You may like to choose a Christmas or Advent carol which gives us a picture of Mary. Play this on a tape recorder and ask people to think of the image that it gives us of Mary as they listen to it.

To finish, someone reads the following litany to Mary. Ask the reader to pause after each line and invite everyone to join in the response: '**Be with us, Mother of Jesus**'.

Daughter Mary, Woman Mary, Mother Mary:

New prophet, New ark, New woman:

Woman of confidence, Woman of hope, Woman of strength:

Woman of integrity, Woman of truth, Woman of peace:

Woman of justice, Woman of faith, Woman of prayer:

Sojourner woman, Alien woman, Refugee woman:

Woman stranger, Woman victim, Woman survivor:

Woman clothed with the sun, crowned with the stars, the moon at her feet:

Mother love, Mother guide, Mother queen:

Life-giving mother, Nourishing mother, Model mother:

Mother listener, Mother minister, Mother teacher:

Mother pregnant, Unwed mother, Lonely birth-giver:

Waiting mother, Weeping mother, Suffering mother.

Mother of a missing child, Mother of a dead child, Mother of risen life:

Mother of hunger, Mother of pain, Mother of fear:

Mother provider, Mother sustainer, Mother reconciler:

Mother comforter, Mother healer, Mother confessor:

Daughter of Zion, Daughter of exodus, Daughter of the poor:

Bearer of the Word, Anointing of the race, Leader of the Church:

Source of blessing, Courageous witness, Image of the body of Christ:

Alternatively, you may like to read the following verses of Psalm 25 together in a slow and prayerful manner:

> To you, Lord, I lift up my soul,
> O my God.
>
> Lord, make your ways known to me,
> teach me your paths.
> Set me in the way of your truth, and
>   teach me,
> for you are the God who saves me.
>
> All day long I hope in you
> because of your goodness, Lord.
> Remember your kindness, Lord,
> your love, that you showed long ago.
> Do not remember the sins of my
>   youth;
> but rather, with your love remember
>   me.
>
> The Lord is so good, so upright,
> he teaches the way to sinners;
> in all that is right he guides the
>   humble,
> and instructs the poor in his way.
>
> All the Lord's paths are love and truth
> for those who keep his covenant and
>   his decrees.
> For the sake of your name, Lord,
> forgive my guilt, for it is great.
>
> Everyone who fears the Lord
> will be taught the course a man
>   should choose;
> his soul will live in prosperity,
> his children have the land for their
>   own.
> The close secret of the Lord belongs
>   to them who fear him,
> his covenant also, to bring them
>   knowledge.
> (after the *Jersualem Bible*)

'Good night, see you next week, safe home!'

Additional background notes for the leaders:

Who was Luke?

Luke was the companion of Paul on some of his missionary journeys, meriting a mention as the 'beloved physician' in the letter to the Colossians. He may have been a native of Antioch or Philippi. A convert from paganism to Christianity, he was probably a doctor and certainly a man of considerable scholarship and culture. For example, he could write excellent Greek, unlike his fellow evangelists! The evidence of his gospel, combined with its second volume – the Acts of the Apostles – shows him to be a capable historian by the standards of his day. Throughout both volumes, too, he demonstrates an extraordinarily detailed knowledge of the Greek Old Testament. Otherwise, little is known of Luke. It seems he was modest to a fault: keen to avoid clearly referring to himself in his own works, and even bashful about his medical knowledge.

The time and place

Luke could have collected the material for his gospel while spending two years with Paul in Caesarea. This early version very probably began at what is now chapter 3. Several scholars feel that Luke very carefully added many more details until his first full gospel eventually saw the light of day in Rome, after the fall of Jerusalem, some time in the 70s AD. Chapters 1 and 2 (which are referred to as the *Lucan Infancy Narrative*) were probably added *after* the rest of the gospel was completed. It helps if we keep this in mind: for these chapters are NOT just an 'opening' but also a 'winding up' of all the gospel's major themes.

The Message

Luke dedicates both his volumes to Theophilus, presumably a Gentile convert like himself. However, he is writing for the benefit of a wider audience: Gentiles as a group; the despised Samaritans; women; the poor, the outcast and the sinner. Above all, Luke is a *universalist*, i.e. he wishes to stress that the Good News of God's compassionate love is for *all* people.

Many of these ideas are present in the Infancy Narrative. The descent of Jesus from Adam (and not from Abraham) emphasizes Jesus' significance for *all* mankind; and the child Jesus, presented in the Temple, is 'a light to enlighten the Gentiles': i.e. he is born to save us *all*. The poor shepherds also have a privileged place in receiving the Good News of the saviour's birth, and, of course, the child himself is born among the destitute poor. Mary, in her turn, proclaims the Lord's greatness: 'Because he has . . . raised up the lowly.'

Allusions to the *Holy Spirit* are frequent in the gospel and Acts. Within the Infancy Narrative the most obvious reference is the virginal conception by the power of the Holy Spirit. However, the activity of the Holy Spirit is also closely linked to the first moment of John the Baptist's existence; Elizabeth is inspired by the Holy Spirit to recognize Mary as the Mother of the Lord; and her husband, Zechariah, filled with the Holy Spirit, prophesies. Finally, while the disciples await the coming of the Holy Spirit as their ascending Lord had promised, Mary, upon whom the Holy Spirit had come at the moment of the conception of Jesus, is with the disciples in prayer. The birth of the church and the birth of the Messiah are both the fruit of the Holy Spirit.

SESSION 3: Worksheet

In the days of King Herod of Judaea there lived a priest called Zechariah who belonged to the Abijah section of the priesthood, and he had a wife, Elizabeth by name, who was a descendant of Aaron. Both were upright in the sight of God and impeccably carried out all the commandments and observances of the Lord. But they were childless: Elizabeth was barren and they were both advanced in years.

Now it happened that it was the turn of his section to serve, and he was exercising his priestly office before God when it fell to him by lot, as the priestly custom was, to enter the Lord's sanctuary and burn incense there. And at the hour of incense all the people were outside, praying.

Then there appeared to him the angel of the Lord, standing on the right of the altar of incense. The sight disturbed Zechariah and he was overcome with fear. But the angel said to him, 'Zechariah, do not be afraid, for your prayer has been heard. Your wife Elizabeth is to bear you a son and you shall name him John. He will be your joy and delight and many will rejoice at his birth, for he will be great in the sight of the Lord; he must drink no wine, no strong drink; even from his mother's womb he will be filled with the Holy Spirit, and he will bring back many of the Israelites to the Lord their God. With the spirit and power of Elijah, he will go before him *to reconcile fathers to their children* and the disobedient to the good sense of the upright, preparing for the Lord a people fit for him.'

In the sixth month the angel Gabriel was sent by God to a town in Galilee called Nazareth, to a virgin betrothed to a man named Joseph, of the House of David; and the virgin's name was Mary. He went in and said to her, 'Rejoice, you who enjoy God's favour! The Lord is with you.' She was deeply disturbed by these words and asked herself what this greeting could mean, but the angel said to her, 'Mary, do not be afraid; you have won God's favour. Look! You are to conceive in your womb and bear a son, and you must name him Jesus. He will be great and will be called Son of the Most High. The Lord God will give him the throne of his ancestor David; he will rule over the House of Jacob for ever and his reign will have no end.'

Feel the word

What strikes you most about the passage?

Who do you feel more sympathy for: Elizabeth or Mary?

How must Mary have felt?

What do the words 'You have found favour with God' say to you?

Explore the word

Do these points help explain the passages at all?

Do they open any new insights?

Responding to the word

Both passages speak of a fearful awareness of God's presence. Do you ever feel like this?

Mary's faith in God's power is astounding. Are you confident of God's power in your life?

Look again at the description of Mary's Son in verses 32 and 33 ('He will be great . . . no end'). Are we ready to welcome that kind of Saviour this Christmas?

How can we make steps to put 'Christ' back into 'Christmas'?

What do Elizabeth and Mary teach us of the dignity of women?

Prayer

We have a moment of quiet to collect our thoughts. Somebody reads a short passage.

After another time of reflection, we finish by praying the following litany of Mary. After each line, the reader will pause and we all respond: **'Be with us, Mother of Jesus'**.

Daughter Mary, Woman Mary, Mother
  Mary:
New prophet, New ark, New woman:
Woman of confidence, Woman of
  hope, Woman of strength:
Woman of integrity, Woman of truth,
  Woman of peace:
Woman of justice, Woman of faith,
  Woman of prayer:
Sojourner woman, Alien woman,
  Refugee woman:
Woman stranger, Woman victim,
  Woman survivor:
Woman clothed with the sun,
  crowned with the stars, the moon at
  her feet:
Mother love, Mother guide, Mother
  queen:
Life-giving mother, Nourishing
  mother, Model mother:
Mother listener, Mother minister,
  Mother teacher:
Mother pregnant, Unwed mother,
  Lonely birth-giver:
Waiting mother, Weeping mother,
  Suffering mother.
Mother of a missing child, Mother of a
  dead child, Mother of risen life:
Mother of hunger, Mother of pain,
  Mother of fear:
Mother provider, Mother sustainer,
  Mother reconciler:
Mother comforter, Mother healer,
  Mother confessor:
Daughter of Zion, Daughter of
  exodus, Daughter of the poor:
Bearer of the Word, Anointing of the
  race, Leader of the Church:
Source of blessing, Courageous
  witness, Image of the body of
  Christ:

To you, Lord, I lift up my soul,
O my God.

Lord, make your ways known to me,
teach me your paths.
Set me in the way of your truth, and
  teach me,
for you are the God who saves me.

All day long I hope in you
because of your goodness, Lord.
Remember your kindness, Lord,
your love, that you showed long ago.
Do not remember the sins of my
  youth;
but rather, with your love remember
  me.

The Lord is so good, so upright,
he teaches the way to sinners;
in all that is right he guides the
  humble,
and instructs the poor in his way.

All the Lord's paths are love and truth
for those who keep his covenant and
  his decrees.
For the sake of your name, Lord,
forgive my guilt, for it is great.

Everyone who fears the Lord
will be taught the course a man
  should choose;
his soul will live in prosperity,
his children have the land for their
  own.
The close secret of the Lord belongs
  to them who fear him,
his covenant also, to bring them
  knowledge.
(after the *Jerusalem Bible*)

Alternatively, you may like to read the
following verses of Psalm 25 together in a
slow and prayerful manner:

SESSION 4:   Leader's Notes

1. Welcome   (5 mins)
(This session will probably take place after Christmas)

Welcome people back to the final evening in the series: 'Tonight we will be exploring the Magnificat, or as some people call it "Mary's manifesto".'

'I would just like to ask you, "What was the best thing about Christmas this year for you?" Have a word with your neighbour.' . . . Then ask people to share their comments in the large group.

'Let's begin with a prayer.'

Father of love,
you made a new creation
through Jesus Christ your Son.
May his coming free us from sin
and renew his life within us,
for he lives and reigns with you and
 the Holy Spirit,
one God, for ever and ever.

2. Involving exercise   (5 mins)

'Do you remember the song "If I ruled the world"? If you wanted to become ruler of the world, what would you promise in order to be elected?'

Invite people to share their thoughts in twos and threes and then to offer their thoughts in the larger groups.

3. Hear the word   (5 mins)

Firstly, the entire passage is read by a woman reader. Then everyone proclaims together verses 51–53 (these are the verses in bold type). Now invite everyone to stand in a circle facing outwards and to proclaim verses 51–53 again together.

4. Feel the word   (*20 mins*)

Invite people to turn their chairs round into groups of threes and fours to reflect on the questions under the heading *FEEL THE WORD* on the worksheet. Encourage the groups to share their feelings and reactions.

What strikes you most about the tone of this passage?

How do you think Mary felt when she proclaimed this hymn of praise?

At first hearing, does this passage make me feel a) threatened, b) thrilled, c) confused?

After about 15 minutes call everyone back together and invite them to share what they were saying in their small group. You do not need to spend longer than about five minutes doing this.

5. Explore the word   (*30 mins*)

'Let's look at the background to this passage and see what Luke meant when he wrote it. There are a few points that may be helpful:'

The Leader then gives a *short* talk based on the points that are laid out below. This does not need to be longer than 5–10 minutes.

This is Mary's great set piece in Luke's Infancy Narrative. We call it the 'Magnificat' from the first word in the Latin translation of it. Like so many other previous passages in the Infancy Narrative, the key which unlocks the full meaning of Mary's hymn of praise lies in the Old Testament. In fact, the Magnificat is like a mosaic made up of dozens of fragments of Old Testament texts; although, above all, it is similar to the Song of Hannah in 1 Samuel 2:1–10. (Hannah, a long-childless lady, miraculously conceives Samuel. Overjoyed, she sings a great hymn of praise.)

Luke also copies the device of many of the psalmists who pass quite naturally from their individual concerns to the concerns of the nation for which they were spokesmen. Likewise, Mary sings of her own exaltation as typical of the new order which is to open out for the *whole* people of God through the coming of her Son. Most striking of all is the fact that Mary foresees her Son's mission as *already accomplished* (that is the sense of the repeated word 'has' in verses 51, 52 and 53).

Make no mistake: we have in Mary's hymn a manifesto fit for any social, political or economic revolution. Luke is fond of what we call 'reversal motifs' (e.g. Lazarus ends up rich; the hated Samaritan exercises real Christian charity). Here in the Magnificat Luke gives full reign to his radical Christian 'topsy-turveydom'. For centuries before Jesus' birth, only collaborators could be rich and powerful, e.g. the Pharisees were notorious collaborators with the Romans. In contrast, the 'poor' were hard-up *and* totally alienated from a corrupt and sinful system imposed from outside. They trusted in God *alone* for their ultimate deliverance; theirs was poverty in every sense.

Jesus' conception in Mary's womb gives direct rise to this extraordinary outburst. In his ministry he was to take up this hope of a new order and rid it of the self-centred nationalism which can so often turn idealism into bigotry. In the Magnificat we have the manifesto of a revolution far more radical than the Jews had ever bargained for.

Luke's gospel does full justice to Mary's feelings expressed here. Unfortunately, we Christians have found Mary's hymn rather strong meat!

Invite people to return to their informal groups and to share their reactions to the input:

Do these points help explain the passage at all?

Do they open up any new insights?

After they have been discussing in groups for about 15 minutes, call everyone back together and take a few responses.

6. Responding to the word (*25 mins*)

Ask people to turn their chairs around again and to share on the questions that they will find under *RESPONDING TO THE WORD* on their worksheets.

Are we preparing/did we prepare for Christmas with the needs of the poor in mind?

Am I in any way vulnerable? If so, do I ever risk admitting it?

As a community/parish are we living out the 'alternative' values urged by the Magnificat?

The song of Mary seems to imply rejection of others and even violence. What do you make of this?

What is more effective in feeding the hungry – Friday self-denial (Lent fasting) or study of the root cause?

After about 20 minutes draw the group together again and invite any sharing in the wider group for about 5 minutes.

7. Prayer

Invite people to quieten down and to focus on the presence of the Lord amongst us. Someone reads this passage:

The Cry for Freedom

The cry for freedom does not just resonate through humanity and nature. It is also God's own cry, for our God identifies himself with his people and his creation. The groans of his Spirit can be heard in the groans of the starving, his Spirit agonizes in the agony of the imprisoned and suffers silently in the mute suffering of nature. Our God is not an apathetic God who, satisfied and pleased with himself, now complacently sleeps in heaven. On the contrary, he is a compassionate God who suffers with us precisely because he loves. His Spirit suffers with his people in the exile, in the ghetto and in the throes of persecution. He suffers with his enslaved creation. Because God created nature as a game of his love for joy, his Spirit is moved by the long history of suffering in the world and participates in this suffering. His Spirit too hungers and cries for freedom.

Jurgen Moltmann

Have a few minutes' quiet, maybe with some background music. A focal point may be helpful – a picture, a candle or a 'holy table'. You could invite people to share a prayer with the group if they wished.

Finish by saying together John Shea's version of the Magnificat:

MAGNIFICAT

All that I am
sings of the God
who brings his life
to birth in me.
My spirit soars
on the wings of my Lord.
He has smiled on me
and the blaze of his smile
no woman or man
shall ever forget.

My God is a gentle strength
who has caught me up
and carried me to greatness.
His love
space cannot hold
nor time age
and all quicken to his touch.

My God is a torrent of justice.
He takes the straight paths
in the minds of the proud
and twists them to labyrinth.
The boot of the oppressor
he pushes aside
and raises the lowly,
whom he loves,
from the ground.
With his own hands
he sets a table for the hungry
but the unfeeling rich
suffer the cold eye
of his judgment.

Our mothers and our fathers
he has held in his arms
and the future grows
like this child within me
for the God of whom I sing
bears us his son.

SESSION 4: Worksheet

The Magnificat

And Mary said:

My soul proclaims the greatness of
the Lord
and my spirit rejoices in God my
Saviour;
because he has looked upon the
humiliation of his servant.
Yes, from now onwards all
generations will call me blessed,
for the Almighty has done great
things for me.
Holy is his name,
and his faithful love extends age after
age to those who fear him.
**He has used the power of his arm,
he has routed the arrogant of
heart.
He has pulled down princes from
their thrones and raised high the
lowly.
He has filled the starving with
good things, sent the rich away
empty.**
He has come to the help of Israel his
servant, mindful of his faithful love
– according to the promise he made
to our ancestors –
of his mercy to Abraham and to his
descendants for ever.

Feel the word

What strikes you most about the tone of this
passage?

How do you think Mary felt when she
proclaimed this hymn of praise?

At first hearing, does this passage make me
feel a) threatened, b) thrilled, c) confused?

Explore the word

Do these points help explain the passage at
all?

Do they open up any new insights?

From *O come, O come Emmanuel* © Bible Reading Fellowship 1990

Responding to the word

Are we preparing/did we prepare for Christmas with the needs of the poor in mind?

Am I in any way vulnerable? If so, do I ever risk admitting it?

As a community/parish are we living out the 'alternative' values urged by the Magnificat?

The song of Mary seems to imply rejection of others and even violence. What do you make of this?

What is more effective in feeding the hungry – Friday self-denial (Lenten fasting) or study of the root cause?

Prayer

We have a few moments of quiet before someone reads a short passage.

We have another period of quiet reflection in which people are welcome to share a prayer with the rest of the group.

We finish by saying together John Shea's Magnificat:

All that I am
sings of the God
who brings his life
to birth in me.
My spirit soars
on the wings of my Lord.
He has smiled on me
and the blaze of his smile
no woman or man
shall ever forget.

My God is a gentle strength
who has caught me up
and carried me to greatness.
His love
space cannot hold
nor time age
and all quicken to his touch.

My God is a torrent of justice.
He takes the straight paths
in the minds of the proud
and twists them to labyrinth.
The boot of the oppressor
he pushes aside
and raises the lowly,
whom he loves,
from the ground.
With his own hands
he sets a table for the hungry
but the unfeeling rich
suffer the cold eye
of his judgment.

Our mothers and our fathers
he has held in his arms
and the future grows
like this child within me
for the God of whom I sing
bears us his son.

D.I.Y. SCRIPTURE SESSIONS

Seven steps in breaking the word of God

Have you enjoyed leading these sessions? Would you like to continue exploring scripture with groups? If so, why not have a go at preparing your own sessions? And don't say 'Impossible', because it is much easier than you may think . . .

The process that we have followed in this pack is very simple. The real beauty of it is that you can easily adapt it to the needs of your particular group and to your own knowledge of the scriptures. This means that you can prepare very useful and enjoyable scripture sessions even if you do not have a great knowledge of the scriptures and their background.

The seven steps that we have followed in this pack are:

1. *Welcome*

2. *Short involving exercise*

3. *Hear the Word*

4. *Feel the Word*

5. *Explore the Word*

6. *Responding to the Word*

7. *Prayer*

Let's walk through this process step by step so that we can see what is involved:

1. Welcome

We welcome people to the evening and generally put them at ease. We start with a short prayer to remind ourselves that we are in the presence of God, that the Holy Spirit is at work amongst us.

2. Short involving exercise

This is just a five minutes exercise which serves a number of purposes:

i) It 'breaks the ice' and gets people talking to each other. This is because we learn by sharing with each other and not just by thinking on our own.

ii) It gets us involved in the theme of the evening. It roots the theme of the evening in our life-experience.

The easiest way to prepare this step is to read the scripture passage that you are going to use and to ask yourself: '**What are the main images or ideas or experiences that this passage is talking about?**' For example in this series week 1 was to do with signs; week 2 with fleeing; week 3 with good news and week 4 with power.

Once we have done this, we then try and think of a way to get people to think about this image or experience. There are many ways of doing this. Often a simple question will do – What's been good news for you this week? A short story can be a good way of involving people in the mood of a scripture passage: e.g. the story of an El Salvadorean woman fleeing from the army. Visual images like posters, slides and even videos are worth bearing in mind also.

3. Hear the Word

The text is read aloud by somebody. People are invited to listen to the word being read rather than following it on the sheet. You may like to think about 'dramatizing' the reading by having different voices read different parts of the passage.

4. Feel the Word

The purpose of this step is to try and get inside the mood or feel of the passage. In this way, we remember that the Word of God is living and active. We are not at this stage interested in asking what the passage meant when it was first written, or what it means now. Instead of exploring the passage in a 'heady' way we want to explore it with our feelings and our 'heart'.

The basic questions that we ask at this stage are things like:

Which words or phrases strike us? Why?

How do the various characters in the story feel?
Why do they do and say the things that they do?

Which of the characters do we identify with? Why?

Obviously we will want to adapt these basic questions to the particular passage that we are looking at. The easiest way to prepare this step is to go through the passage slowly and reflectively, asking the questions above. In this way you can put flesh onto the bones of these questions: e.g. you might want to ask what a particular word or phrase says to the group; you may want to focus on a particular character in the story and to ask how they felt at a particular moment.

5. Explore the Word

The purpose of this step is to explore a little of the background to the passage. The scriptures were written in a very different culture from our own; often points can seem strange and can hide the meaning of the passage.

By exploring the background of the passage, we move away from focussing on our feelings and the mood of the passage and we turn to ask what the passage meant to its first hearers.

People sometimes feel intimidated by this step because they feel that it demands specialized scripture knowledge. However, this is not so. In this step we are not looking for very detailed and difficult background knowledge. In fact difficult and detailed knowledge would be unhelpful for the group. We are much more interested in exploring a few simple background points that can be gathered very easily.

Here are four simple ways to explore the background of any scripture passage:

i) **Look at the context**
   Look at where this passage comes in the book that it is taken from.
   Look at what place it occupies in the overall story. Ask yourself:
   What happens before this passage?
   What happens after this passage?
   Does this help us understand what is happening in the passage?

ii) **Use the footnotes**
   Especially in the Jerusalem or New Jerusalem Bible, the footnotes often explain obscure words or phrases in a passage.

iii) **Look up the references in the margin**
   These refer to other scripture passages with the same themes, or to the source of quotations in the passage, and help to show what was in the mind of the writer.

iv) **Use other accessible sources**, for example:
   – the introductions to each book in the Jerusalem or New Jerusalem Bible;
   – *Guidelines*, regular readings arranged in weekly units; combines excellent scripture study with a very accessible and readable approach; details from the Bible Reading Fellowship (see address in this book, behind title-page).

– E. Charpentier, *How to read the Old Testament, How to read the New Testament* (both SCM Press).

6. Responding to the Word

The purpose of this step is to re-focus on our own situation and to ask how this passage challenges us and calls us to new life. In doing this we remember that the Word is living and active, that at the end of the day we study scripture in order to learn more about how God is present, calling us to new life today. And we remember that this challenge comes to us both as individuals and communities.

The basic questions that we ask are:

What does this passage say to our situation?

How does it challenge us – as individuals?
                                      – as parish?
                                      – as nation?

What action or changes does this call us to make as individuals and as communities?

As with step four, these questions have to be 'played with' and adapted to the particular passage that we are exploring.

7. Prayer

We finish with a time of prayer. We do this in order to focus on the Lord's call to us to enter more deeply into the freedom of his life. There are a few simple movements that are useful to remember:

i) Settle down

We take a moment to quieten ourselves, to become aware of the Lord's presence amongst us. It is helpful to change the atmosphere: to dim the lighting (?); to move the chairs into a circle; to play some soft music. It is a good idea to invite people to put down any papers, bags, etc. that they are holding. It is also useful to have a visual focus: this could be a candle; a slide; a poster or icon; an appropriate symbol; you may even like to prepare a 'holy table'.

ii) A short reading

Choose a reading that draws together some of the themes for the evening. Remember that you do not need to be confined to scripture readings.

iii) A time of quiet reflection

It may be helpful to play a tape of meditative music; many people like the Taizé chants. Or you could play a tape of an appropriate song and invite people to reflect on the words. You may like to invite the people to share any informal prayers with the group if they wished.

iv) Do something together

Finish by doing something together: singing a hymn; saying a well-known prayer together; reading a short passage.

ACKNOWLEDGEMENTS

Darton, Longman & Todd Ltd and Double-day & Co. Inc. for biblical quotations, from *The Jerusalem Bible* © 1966, 1967 and 1968 and *The New Jerusalem Bible* © 1985.

William Collins Sons & Co. for 'The True Christmas' from O. Romero, *The Church is all of us*.

Latinamerican Press for 'Like Mary, I too had to flee'.

Pax Christi for quotations from 'Raids on the Unspeakable' in *Thomas Merton on Peacemaking and Nonviolence*.

Albatross Books and Lion Publishing for David Hewitson's 'Like your landlord . . .' from *Christianity made simple: Belief*, 1983.

Amnesty International for Salvador de Madariaga's 'For those who grasp their prison bars'.

Christian Conference for Asia for Elizabeth Tapia's 'Who am I?'

OCP Publications, Oregon USA for James Hensen's 'A Litany of Mary' from *Litany: When the Church gathers*.

Jurgen Moltmann for 'The cry for freedom'.

Argus Communications, Texas USA for John Shea's 'Magnificat' from *The God who fell from heaven*, 1979.

The Bible Reading Fellowship was founded 'to encourage the systematic and intelligent reading of the Bible, to emphasize its spiritual message and to take advantage of new light shed on Holy Scripture'.

Over the years the Fellowship has proved a trustworthy guide for those who want an open, informed and contemporary approach to the Bible. It retains a sense of the unique authority of Scripture as a prime means by which God communicates.

As an ecumenical organization, the Fellowship embraces all Christian traditions and its readers are to be found in most parts of the world.